THE PURPLE JEEP

A COUPLE'S STORY OF LOVING THROUGH DYING

LINDA HUFFSTETLER-DEARING

CITIOFBOOKS, INC.
3736 Eubank NE Suite A1
Albuquerque, NM 87111-3579
www.citiofbooks.com
Hotline: 1 (877) 389-2759
Fax: 1 (505) 930-7244

Ordering Information:

Quantity sales. Special discounts are available on quantity purchases by corporations, associations, and others. For details, contact the publisher at the address above.

Printed in the United States of America.

ISBN-13:   Softcover   979-8-89391-148-0
                eBook   979-8-89391-149-7

Library of Congress Control Number: 2024910924

TABLE OF CONTENTS

In memory of
Maurice Eugene Huffstetler-Dearing
May 24, 1944-February 2, 2001

Preface

I think it is the nature of losing a loved one to feel that no matter what you did to help, it wasn't enough. I loved my husband and stood by him during two catastrophic illnesses within an eighteen-month period. I advocated for him in the medical community when he was too sick to speak for himself. I fed him, changed his dressings, listened to his sorrows and regrets, and applauded every small achievement, yet today I still feel that somehow, I could have done a better job.

This story is for every loving caregiver, for every friend who has felt, "If only I had done more, I could have made a difference." We are all brothers and sisters in our grief—and in our love. In the weaving together of all our stories into one, may we find peace.

Linda L. Huffstetler-Dearing

Surviving Spouse

Introduction

After getting our eight-year-old daughter off to school each morning, I'd return to Gene in our bed, the "big bed" we always called it. Gene wasn't in the hospital bed yet. We would hold each other's hands and talk for hours. As counselors, we used words to help us try and make sense of what was happening in our lives. We needed to put into some perspective Gene's debilitating illness, which was eating away at him on the inside and eating away at the fabric of our family lives on the outside. Mostly, we talked about the future—our future if Gene lived, because we couldn't give up hope; my future if Gene died, because we couldn't live a lie.

I am writing this story in the hope that others in similar circumstances will be able to see themselves and their loved ones in a new way. Many times, the stress and busyness of our lives rob us of mindfulness and clarity in how we deal with one another. After registering Gene in hospice, we expected him to live at least another six months. Within three weeks of registering him in hospice, I resigned from my position as an educator at the local hospital in order to take care of him full time at home. I am grateful every day that I didn't delay that decision until it was too late. Gene died almost two months to the day after being registered into hospice.

One message I want to convey to you is that none of us know how long we have together, and that is especially true when a loved one has a terminal illness. We must keep hope alive, always, but we can also act as though each day is the last we'll have together. Sometimes our sense of desperation keeps us from believing in the seriousness of our loved one's condition. Acting as if everything is just fine helps us cope.

In fifteen years of being in and around hospice care as a volunteer, there is only one rule I've seen applied consistently in all the various programs: Everyone has the right to experience their loss in their own way.

This story isn't a template for anyone else. Yet, for those of you who are losing someone dear to you, I hope it can give you permission to let go of at least some of your fear, so that you can give and receive as much from the relationship as you can bear. My own experience showed me how painful it is to truly be in the present moment with my husband, and to love him, knowing that at any moment he could be gone.

My experience working with bereavement, as a counselor and as a respite care giver volunteer for hospice programs, has given me a window into peoples' lives. I've seen tremendous courage in the face of desperate loss. I have also seen people afraid to reach out and make emotional or physical contact with their loved ones. Oh, what opportunities have been lost because of the assumption that "there's nothing I can do about it" or "there's nothing I can say that will make a difference." Gene's greatest fear when he learned of his cancer diagnosis was that people would treat him like "a dead man walking," as he put it. He was afraid that people would no longer meet his eyes, would avoid physical contact with him, or would avoid him altogether. In some cases, that's exactly what happened. In other cases, after learning of Gene's illness, people went out of their way to be kind, to make contact with him, and even to say their final goodbyes. His children came and sat with him during his final month, and in the end, those personal connections were the most meaningful to Gene.

Many books have been written regarding why people in our culture avoid thinking about death and dying. My story does not try to address the whys. I want to share our story about how we experienced Gene's illnesses and his death.

I hope this will be helpful in opening you to your own experience, so that you can be more emotionally and physically present for yourself and your loved one.

This is our story.

Linda Huffstetler-Dearing

Meeting Each Other

One sunny fall afternoon as my daughter and I were riding together in the car she asked me, "Mommy, are you going to get married again?" There was a long pause as I thought about how to answer her for the hundredth time.

"Honey," I told her, "It would take a very special man to make me happy. At my age, you know exactly what you want. He would have to have the soul of an artist and the spirit of a warrior. He'd have to ride a Harley. And what else?"

"A Jeep!"

"Yes! And what color jeep? What's my favorite color? "Purple," she shot back.

"Yep! A purple Jeep Wrangler." We laughed at our silliness and went on our way, completely unaware...

"Two weeks later, Gene Dearing rode into my life on a Harley." As I stood in front of the crowd of family and friends assembled for Gene's Memorial Service, recalling this conversation with my daughter. I smiled. "This is a true love story."

I was struck first by how handsome he was. Leather chaps, vest, even a "Harley" kerchief wrapped around his head. *Bet this guy's all beauty, no brains,* I thought as I watched him dismount. I had let myself be talked into a blind date. He was taking off his leathers as he walked towards me, greeting me for the first time with a hug. There was something about his blue eyes, something so familiar. Sitting in my kitchen, we spent the next twenty-three hours talking to each other. We talked about everything, most especially living life to the fullest and raising children well. Everything important we could think of, we said to each other. And we laughed and laughed, until our bellies ached. We could hardly breathe for the joy of finding each other, at last.

Eighteen hours later he was back, having asked me out on a date for the next day. He drove up in his Wrangler. *His purple Jeep Wrangler.* We were going to the mountain, to one of my favorite spots. I was clutching Shelley, Eliot, and Whitman; he carried a supply of string cheese and Fuji applies. Sitting midway up the hill, overlooking a pond, we sat on a blanket listening to the whispering of the pine trees. I read poetry to him and saw him cry for the first time. In time I was to learn more about him: he was a silver artist of fifteen years with artwork in collections all over the country. He was a substance-abuse counselor working with alcoholics and addicts. A decorated war hero, he was a marine whose war wounds were so severe he had never recovered. He was still a marine—a gentle soul with a warrior's spirit.

Losing all sense of time on the mountain, we were late and had to rush to get back. We would be home, he promised, before my daughter got home from school. We pulled up just before her school bus stopped. No time to hide him now! She walked over to us.

First, she looked at me, then at him. I tried to introduce them, but with the knowing sense of a child, she stepped between us. With wide eyes looking at the jeep, she put her hands on her hips.

"We don't live here," she said. "This isn't our house. We live down the street." The gauntlet was thrown down. He laughed out loud.

"I know where you live, Hollis," he said to her, smiling. "It's going to be all right."

One Morning

I remember the day Gene and I were leaving on a trip up to Northern Arizona, to the pines. This was our first extended trip together.

Our hiking adventure would include a few days in the mountains at a private bed-and-breakfast resort. We were packing the jeep. He was coming down the stairs; I was on my way up. We met under the arch-way in the dining room and stopped, caught in each other's eyes. He put down the suitcases and held me in his arms, looking at me, and I felt a field of warmth surround us. There was music playing in the background, though nothing was "on." We were held in the moment, transported out of time, swaying to the music. Every now and then, one of us would say, "We have to go," "We have to pack," "We have reservations." But neither of us moved away. We were held together and stayed like that for almost three hours. Locked in each other's eyes.

Our "marriage" happened in those moments. A joining of our hearts in a way so profound we could never explain it afterwards. I have a photograph that the innkeeper took of us that weekend. Joined together, silent, looking out onto a lake covered with snow, there was already a peace between us.

The Emergency Room

My husband was shouting at me, "I'm dying, Linda! Something is killing me. I don't know what, but I'm getting my backpack. I'm leaving!" My husband of eight months, who'd never raised his voice to me, looked at my shattered face and softened.

"Linda, I don't know what's wrong with me. Maybe it's being married again. Maybe all the stress of commuting. Whatever it is, I've got to get out of here." He crumpled onto the bed, staring at me with wild eyes.

I woke up many times during the night. Reaching out instinctively to touch him, I found him missing. The warmth that always surrounded us, keeping us close, was being stretched to the limit. I felt him with me but couldn't see him. Sometimes he had nightmares and got up to sit in his chair downstairs, in the dark, chasing the demons out of his mind from a war fought long ago, now over. I'd go back to sleep.

Fully awake now, listening to my husband's desperation, I felt helpless. I'd never seen him so angry. He'd never lashed out at me before. "I've been up all night, Linda, bleeding." Looking at his ashen face, I realized he was scared.

"I'm calling the hospital, Gene," I said, reaching for the phone. He put up no resistance and a fear grew in the pit of my stomach. I called the TLC line at the VA Medical Center in a larger town two hours away. Talking to a triage nurse, I explained.

"My husband has ulcerative colitis. He's been seeing the GI docs there for five months. He's been bleeding the whole time. He's on Prednisone, but it isn't helping. He bled again all night. Please help us. What should we do?"

"Get him in the car and bring him down here to the Life Support Unit," she advised me. I looked at my husband sitting on the bed, sweaty face in his hands, shaking.

"I don't think he can make it two hours," I told her.

"Well, then take him to any emergency room that's close."

Putting down the phone, I took charge. "We're going to the ER here, Gene. I'm calling Jane to pick up Hollis. We'll leave as soon as she's gone."

Within fifteen minutes, we were on our way to the hospital. I felt strangely disoriented, out of my body, looking at "us" from outside myself. My husband had always been *my* protector. Now he was sick and I was acting like a mother with a child, telling him what to do, guiding *him*. It all felt unreal and unfamiliar to me. *What's happening?* I wondered. *What's happening to our family? I don't like this. I don't like these changes at all.* Being a mental-health counselor with a healthy family, I had little experience dealing with physical illness. My daughter was rarely sick, and had never even broken anything. I had never even been to an emergency room.

At the local emergency room, we were taken immediately to a bed. After taking his vital signs, the nurse put Gene on an IV and I was asked to complete the admission forms. After consulting with the VA Medical Center, the doctor in the Emergency Room gave Gene a pint of blood and ordered X-rays and a culture. Then they said he could go home.

Over the next three months, Gene continued to bleed internally. He attended two and sometimes three appointments a week at the VA Medical Center two hours away from our home. He also continued his work, commuting four hours a day to his job as a substance-abuse counselor in another town. Nothing the GI doctors recommended helped the bleeding. His treatment consisted mostly of ever-increasing doses of steroids. Gene had begun to lose weight, and four months after the visit to the local emergency room he had lost almost fifty pounds. Frustrated with his worsening condition, I accompanied Gene to one of his doctor's visits at the GI clinic. After relating my frustration and concerns to the doctor, he told us that it was no doubt my aggressiveness that was aggravating my husband's condition! His only medical advice, other than increasing the steroids, was that perhaps Gene should go back to smoking cigarettes, since in case studies nicotine was shown to calm down the colon. After months of trying, Gene had finally been able to quit smoking about eight months before this doctor's visit. Neither of us considered the doctor's insights into our relationship or his "medical advice" very helpful.

We had arranged to have his primary physician changed to the physician's assistant at the local VA clinic, to cut down on the traveling time. One morning, after eight months of continuous bleeding, dozens of outpatient doctor's appointments, and several visits to the Life Support Unit for transfusions, he appeared for his regularly scheduled visit with his new primary care giver. She took his vital signs and called to admit him into the hospital at the VA Medical Center. That afternoon, I drove him to the VA Medical Center two hours away.

The Surgery

The day after he was admitted to the hospital, Gene was losing more blood rectally than the medical team could pump into him intravenously. The attending physician, medical students, and GI surgeons were called in to collaborate on a treatment plan. We were told that had Gene not been hospitalized when he was, there was a good possibility he would have bled out during the night. I spent as much time at the hospital as possible, trying to keep our daughter's school and activity schedule in our hometown as close to normal as I could.

Working full time, commuting back and forth to the hospital, and dealing with the stress of medical unknowns wore on me, but nothing prepared me for my visits with Gene. Watching his physical and psychological deterioration created a sense of helplessness I'd never experienced before. I never knew him to be apathetic and hopeless. He had always been the calming, optimistic presence in our family. I was the nervous, high-powered driver, Gene the calm and loving nurturer. Gene had been in the hospital about a week when we were given our options. A total and permanent ileostomy was the only option available at that medical facility. This would mean his entire colon and rectum would be removed and a hole created in the small intestine for the elimination of wastes. It would mean he would wear a bag on his abdomen for the rest of his life. The only hospital in the VA system that performed the reversible two-step procedure was out of state, in San Francisco. It might take months to get Gene on the list for that procedure, and in the meantime, he would have to go home and wait. The doctors advised that the prognosis for his survival was grim if he waited. After learning of our decision, the doctors scheduled Gene's surgery within a few days. We were assured that a permanent ileostomy was the only curative procedure known for ulcerative colitis.

Gene liked his surgeon, a young man from the local medical school who would be heading the surgical team. It would be this surgeon's first solo ileostomy, without his mentor assisting. He was personable, verbal, and empathetic, always volunteering to answer questions and go over every aspect of the surgery in detail. Five hours after the surgery began, the surgeon found me in the family waiting room.

"The surgery went well," the doctor told me. "The colon was diseased all the way through," he said. "We've sent it to the lab, and the pathology report should be back in a few days. It looked ulcerative, not cancerous, but we won't know for sure until the pathology report comes back." He saw my obvious relief, then he added, "Mrs. Dearing, after I saw that colon, I knew there was no other option. You and Gene made the right decision to take it out." He shook my hand and turned me over to the nurse who was waiting to take me to step-down, where Gene was receiving intensive post-surgical care.

Coming Home

Walking into the kitchen with a bag of groceries, I heard the phone ringing.

"Hello?"

"Honey..." My husband's voice sounded strained over the phone.

"What's going on, Gene?" I was worried. After his colon surgery, Gene had spent a month in the hospital. A week after the surgery, expecting him to be discharged, I hadn't gotten my usual phone call. I called the nurse's station and was told that all of Gene's stitches had burst open with infection. Eight months of Prednisone had rendered his immune system unable to fight off infection, and his surgical incisions weren't healing.

"They're going to discharge me tomorrow, finally. But they're only going to pay for home health nurses to come in two times a week. Other than that, we're on our own."

"Can you walk, Genie?" My once-strong and virile husband had lost over fifty pounds, his hair was falling out, and his poor body was bruised and battered from constant IV tubing and four wound-dressing changes a day.

"I walked to the door today, baby. We'll have to put me on the family room couch until I get stronger."

"We'll manage, Gene. I'll be there in two hours."

When I walked into Gene's hospital room the next morning, he was hooked up to liquid antibiotics by IV tubing and was waiting for the phlebotomist to come and remove the shunt in his neck. I sat by his bed and held his hand, and we talked about what the two-hour car trip back to the house might be like for him. The director of home health walked into the room.

"Mrs. Dearing?" she said, calling me the name the VA used for us, since officially men do not change their names when they get married. "Yes," I answered.

"Has anyone showed you how to change your husband's dressing?" "No. No one has said anything to me about it."

"Well, it's going to be up to you, Mrs. Dearing, four times a day. You might as well come over here and take a look," she said as she beckoned me to Gene's bedside. Standing up, I looked at Gene, who was making a scary face. Pulling out the dressing, she stepped aside and motioned for me to look more closely at his wound. I stepped closer and looked down. Suddenly I felt like I was in a misty fog, everything growing dark around me. I looked at the wound I thought must have been healing (or the doctors wouldn't be sending him home), and I saw Gene's pelvic bone, the incision clean and clear all the way to the bone. I could hardly breathe.

"I don't know if I can do this," I said, sitting down beside Gene on the bed. "I've never seen anything like that before. My specialty is nervous breakdowns." She looked at me with some concern.

"Well, Mrs. Dearing, there's no time like the present to learn. I'm going to give you four-by-fours, gel wound dressing, and long swabs. I want you to smooth the gel on the four-by-fours and pack that wound loosely with the swab. I'm going to watch you do it, because we are discharging Mr. Dearing into your care this morning, and by the time you get home you'll need to dress that wound again. Okay?"

I stood up and with shaky hands began to pull on sterile gloves, like I'd seen his nurses do dozens of times. I took the four-by-fours, the gel wound dressing, and the swab, and I began to pack the hole in my husband's abdomen. Looking into his face, I could see he wasn't sure whether I was up to the task. Gene had received round-the-clock nursing care for six weeks and was now being sent home with his beloved wife, the emotional trauma specialist.

"I sure wish this was a nervous breakdown, Linda," he wisecracked as I packed the wound to the top. Looking around for guidance, I held out my hand and the director handed me some paper tape.

"This goes over everything," she said, and with her hands over mine she showed me how to tape the wound shut.

"The phlebotomist will be here shortly to take the shunt out of Mr. Dearing's neck and he'll be ready to go home." She sounded almost cheerful as she smiled and left the room. My eyes big, I sat by Gene, shaking.

"I didn't know about this part," I said in a low voice, trying not to reveal how scared I was. He shut his eyes and lay back on the bed, no doubt contemplating what the next few weeks would be like.

After the phlebotomist removed all his tubing, we dressed Gene and helped him into a wheelchair. We signed the discharge papers and a large box of wound-care materials was placed into my arms, as Gene was wheeled down to the Life Support Unit exit. The exercise he'd had, consisting of walking to the door, came in handy as he walked to the passenger's side of the car and lay down in the seat. White-faced and buckled in, he nestled into his seat and we drove the two hours home.

The Summer of Hope

Gene had been home three months, and we were down to packing his abdominal wound twice a day. A month into his rehabilitation at home, Gene's rectal site had burst open. A trip to the VA Medical Center revealed that the massive doses of steroids prescribed before the surgery had taken their toll on this wound as well and that it was not properly healing. We began to pack that wound several times a day too. Feeding and cleaning my husband, as well as caring for his wounds, had become another full-time job in my life. I was working full time, running to keep up with Hollis' school and after-school activities, and caring for Gene the rest of the time. My life was characterized by feeling tired and being anxious almost all the time. I awoke every night with a list in my head of things I had to do the next day.

During this time, Gene was very depressed. Many days he would sit in front of the television and watch the news and weather channels. He would be sitting there when I left in the morning and would be in the same position when I would check on him at midday, and again when I arrived home from work in the afternoon. His appetite was still poor, and without a colon, he could not assimilate nutrients. We had to educate ourselves on new and creative ways to nourish him. Every day, we would supplement his two or three small meals with protein drinks. Though he wasn't gaining weight, at least he wasn't continuing to lose any.

He was finicky about his stoma, the hole coming out of his small intestine. As an athlete, he was used to hiking and backpacking for hours and days at a time. He expressed his fear, hopelessness, that in his weakened state he would never be active again. How, he would ask, with all the stuff it was going to take to care for his stoma, could he ever hope to backpack in the wilderness again? Being disabled after his surgery for such an extended time, he had to quit his job. We also had to navigate through mounds of paperwork for the Social Security Administration and Veterans Administration to secure disability income for our family.

Through it all, we were hopeful. We clung to the assurances from the medical professionals that his surgical procedure was curative. Gene would never have another bout of ulcerative colitis and would never have to cope with even the possibility of getting colon cancer. The pathology report on his diseased colon had come back negative for cancer. We were in the clear, and we both believed that in time he would heal from the surgery. Thousands of others had survived this type of surgery. The Internet was full of their testimonials.

Although I was tired and worried most of the time, Gene's depression was something I could cope with. After all, depression was my specialty. This part of Gene's recovery finally gave me something to do, and in some ways it was easier than dealing with the emotional aspect of his illnesses, especially when I felt helpless and could only watch him deteriorate. I went into "social worker mode," helping him manage his medications, writing lists of questions for the doctors, making and keeping follow-up doctor's appointments, and completing all the official forms for disability income.

I remember the day in July when Gene took over his own wound care. He was walking up and down the stairs again and was strong enough to pack his own abdominal wound once a day. Because of the awkward position, I still packed the rectal wound once a day, but we were both elated that we were seeing physical progress. He was taking over more of his own care and was beginning to feel that it was just a matter of time before he was the active, vibrant man he had been before his illness.

I think the most demoralizing part for Gene was looking at his emaciated body in the mirror. His skin sagged and his body was riddled with red pockmarks where the surgery staples had been removed. He related to the old bodybuilding ads in the magazines of our youth and talked continually about looking like the weakling at the beach who was getting sand kicked into his face by the bully. His eyes were sad.

His body drooped. I wondered whom this person was, lying beside me in bed. He looked like a wizened old man.

This was our transition time. We were still trying to adjust to all the changes caused by the ulcerative colitis that had happened so quickly over the past eight months. One day our daughter came home crying after playing with the neighborhood kids. One of her playmates had called Gene "an old geezer." She didn't know what it meant, but it sounded mean to her. We all talked about how old Gene looked now after his illness and surgery. He had aged at least twenty years, looking like a man in his seventies. Since she was seven years old at the time, Gene looked like a very old step-father indeed an old geezer. We made light of it, but in Gene's eyes I could see how serious this was to him, how these dramatic changes in his appearance were eroding his self-esteem.

We had always enjoyed a creative and active sex life, but the debilitating nature of the disease and surgery had left Gene exhausted and insecure. We had been assured that even should the surgery render him medically impotent, the new medication Viagra "would take care of it 100%," as the surgeon had said. As time went on, it became apparent to us both that there had been nerve damage during the surgery and that Gene was faced with impotency. This revelation was devastating to his already suffering self-image. If there was ever a time for a medical miracle, it was now. At his next doctor's appointment, Gene asked for a prescription for Viagra. He was told that this medication was not on the VA formulary. He was handed the script and told we would have to buy it for ourselves.

I remember the night we were going to have our Viagra date. We were like teenagers, as Gene took a pill and waited the recommended hour for it to "work." However, the pill didn't work. We talked for many hours after that night about our feelings and thoughts, about the so-called standards set by our society, and especially about what Gene considered virile and sexy. I often wondered if our experiences were the same as those of other couples whose husbands had been rendered medically impotent from prostate cancer or other diseases. Other than the Internet, we had no sources of reference or support. Our small town didn't have an Osteomate Group, as it is called, but through an organization in a nearby city, we were put in touch with an osteomate living in our town. It was a difficult time for both of us, but especially for Gene.

Throughout early summer, I watched him in the stillness of the afternoons as he sat alone in his easy chair in front of the fireplace, wrestling with his demons and having to redefine himself as a man while grappling with so many losses in his life. Mobility, body image, sexual function, and most especially the inability to take his daily "constitutional," as he called it. He would seek me out afterwards, wanting to talk about what he was thinking and feeling. Fortunately, years of being a counselor had taught him about feelings, and I listened for hours as he began to figure out his new identity in the world.

It was a time of great learning for him as a person and for us as a couple. We were learning that love has no boundaries, no firm definitions. Love encompasses chronic and acute disease and monitors the changes in our lives, soothing even our mutilated bodies. We learned after a while that our love didn't have anything to do with our bodies at all. Love was a beautiful field of energy between us, and my desire for my husband never waned as I experienced, for the first time in my life, a love that went far beyond the beauty of the body. My love and desire for him grew stronger every day as I watched him grow into his new self, a man made of new material, the material of survival, created within the fabric of love and trust.

Gene became freer during this time in his life. He learned to trust me not only with his heart and with his money, as he would have said, *but with his life.*

In late July, we planned our first post-illness camping trip. Gene told me he always wanted to take the Durango to Silverton, Colorado, train ride. We built a three-state camping trip around the train ride. It was during that two-week camping trip that Gene began to reclaim his body. He began to assert his will over his body, rather than allowing his body to assert its will over him. We camped in unimproved campsites, where he would dump his ostomy bag much like he would have dealt with the elimination of his body wastes before the surgery, in some secluded wooded area. He shoveled over it with dirt. He carried his materials to care for his stoma in a little waterproof sack attached to his belt. We began to laugh again, as he started to refer to himself as the Improved Husband, and the Deluxe Model Husband Who Came with Attachments. His ability to face the challenges in his life and to laugh at the changes began to heal him and bring him back to life—and to me. I welcomed him back with open arms.

The Cancer Diagnosis

It was a beautiful late-October morning. Leaves were falling from the pecan trees surrounding our home outside our windows, and our kitchen was bustling with activity. I was cooking breakfast for us and Gene was straightening and blow-drying Hollis' hair, preparing her for school that morning.

"I'm going down to the VA today to pick up my new glasses," Gene said as he pulled Hollis' hair through the brush.

"Oh, continuing with your new-and-improved look, huh?" I said as I came over to kiss him on his cheek.

"Yep. Be prepared, because I'm going to look sexier than ever when I get back." He winked at me, continuing to play hairdresser for his step-daughter. With his health improving every day, his mood was lighter than ever, and he and Hollis were becoming very close again. Being African-American, Hollis was very particular about her hair. She now preferred Gene's hairstyles to mine.

"You might want to stop in at Life Support, Gene, and ask them to check on that cough. I can hear you wheezin' from the other room. How long have you been on antibiotics for that cold?"

"Jeez, it's been what, three months now? I'll drop in if I have time. Since I'll be in the city, do we need anything for Hollis' Halloween costume?" He nudged her arm as he asked.

"Nope. All ready to go," she answered.

After breakfast I dropped Hollis off at school and went to my office. The phone rang a few hours later, while I was creating a new curriculum for my anti-tobacco classes in the local elementary school.

"Hello?"

"Linda, I'm at the VA. Honey, they've admitted me." My heart stopped. Darkness closed in around me and I forced myself to breathe. "What's going on, Gene?"

"Well, I stopped by the LSU after I got my glasses and they took an X-ray."

"What is it? Do you have pneumonia?"

"Well, they don't know, honey. They found a little spot and they need to do more tests. It could be anything, I guess."

"Gene, what's wrong? What are you thinking?"

"Well, I'm thinking, I guess, the worst. That it could be cancer. But they told me it could be anything. A cyst, or a scar from having Valley Fever...you know, anything."

"I'll pick Hollis up and we'll come on down to the hospital as soon as she's out of school. I love you. We'll get through this. We will. You just hang in there, okay? I love you. Bye."

"I love you too, baby," he said as he hung up the phone.

I sat in my work cubicle a long time. Then I walked into my supervisor's office and sat down in a chair by her desk.

"They've found a spot on Gene's lung," I told her, starting to cry. We worked with information dealing with lung cancer, emphysema, and other tobacco-related illnesses every day in our work as health educators. We were part of a statewide team of health educators, specially trained to work with tobacco-use prevention and cessation. My supervisor comforted me, and we talked awhile about what other things it might be, not believing it could be lung cancer. For a little while in her office, I relived the horrors of the past year. Sinking back into disbelief, I took the rest of the day off and prepared for another trip to the VA Medical Center, two hours away from home.

Since Gene had been admitted on a Friday, the additional tests could not be scheduled until after the weekend. Hollis and I stayed at a nearby motel for the weekend, visiting the hospital as much as we could, and then returned home so she could go back to school and I could go back to work.

The next few days were spent in a fog, going through the motions of pulling together Hollis' Halloween costume and just the two of us trick-or-treating in the neighborhood. My mind was constantly wondering what was going on in my husband's hospital room 120 miles away.

We were all scared. A new specter had entered our lives. And though the medical team was hopeful, this time they were vague. Every test was "inconclusive," but "it could be cancer," they would say. "The spot" was encapsulated liquid, we heard, and so other diagnoses had to be ruled out. By Wednesday of the following week, they had performed a bronchoscopy, where they inserted a tube with a camera on the end into his lungs. The doctor who performed the procedure told Gene it looked like he had a form of lung cancer called squamous cell carcinoma. It was a cancer, he said, related to Agent Orange and tobacco use. Had Gene been exposed to Agent Orange in Vietnam? Yes. Had he ever smoked? Yes, for over forty years, until we'd met. He'd been tobacco free just two years. The doctor took a sample for a biopsy and sent it to the lab. Two days later, a resident came into Gene's room to tell him the diagnosis had been confirmed. He had lung cancer, specifically, squamous cell carcinoma. Though the tumor was small and confined to the left lung, it appeared to be inoperable, since it was in the main bronchia leading into the lung. Operating on it might cause it to spread. A new medical team would be in to talk to Gene about his options.

It took almost a week for the medical team to come into Gene's room and talk to him about treatment. During that time, I watched the new life drain out of my husband's face and body as he prepared himself for the onslaught of this new illness. Every day without a medical plan took its toll. I sat by his bed, held his hand, and began my journey as Mrs. Dearing, Husband's Advocate. It started the sixth day after the confirmation of the diagnosis.

"It has been six days!" I was saying loudly at the nurses' station. "Six days and not one person has been in to talk to us about how we are going to treat this cancer. What is going on here? This is cancer. Time is of the essence." I was scared and angry.

"Mrs. Dearing, we are so sorry. You have every right to be upset. We aren't sure who's on call right now. We'll make some calls and find out.

Please go back to Mr. Dearing, and as soon as we talk to a doctor we'll let you know." The nurse sounded sincere.

"No. We have waited long enough! I'm standing right here until you tell me who's in charge of his case now and until I can talk to that person." I stood firm in front of the nurse's desk. She looked at the resolve in my face and started to dial the phone. She paged one doctor after another, asking questions. After about the fourth page, a resident called her back. During the six days since the diagnosis, she relayed to me after she had hung up the phone, the team had changed, since it was the first of the month. Since it was a medical training facility, each month the team changed to provide training for a new set of medical students and residents. The nurse reported that the resident had assured her over the phone that Mr. Dearing's case had been referred to a new oncology resident, who would be in touch with us tomorrow to set up a treatment plan.

"Mrs. Dearing, you have every right to be upset," the nurse said again softly. "I would be, too, but the delay is due mainly to the team change at the start of the month. But the referral has been made to oncology and you will be hearing from the new resident tomorrow. I promise. They are very busy, since they get constant new referrals, but we'll keep reminding them until they come up to talk to you."

I went back to Gene's room. He was curled up into a ball on his side, trying to figure out how to use his new inhaler. Well acquainted with this medication, I showed him how to use it.

"Gene, the medical team has changed, because it's the first of the month. The new oncology resident will be here first thing tomorrow morning to go over the treatment plan." I crawled into bed behind him, putting my arm over his waist. "Go to sleep, honey. I'm not going anywhere until we find out what we have to do next." We fell asleep, weary from all our unanswered questions, dark clouds of fear crowding back into our hearts.

Treatment

The next afternoon, the oncology resident was apologetic. A resident from the University of Arizona Medical Center, he was there to coordinate treatment between that facility and the VA Medical Center. The U of A, he told us, provided radiation treatment for VA patients. Because of the tumor's location, it was probably inoperable. Because of the loss of Gene's colon, he might not be able to assimilate the chemotherapy. The lack of a colon, along with Gene's generally poor medical condition from the major surgery earlier that year, made him a poor candidate for chemotherapy anyway. That left radiation treatments. Gene was to be discharged from the hospital that day and would meet with his VA oncologist in two days, back at the VA Medical Center. At that time, his cancer would be staged, in other words, given a number reflecting the seriousness of his prognosis. Any treatment options would be confirmed during that meeting by the oncologist. He would also be given a bone scan within the week before the meeting with the assigned radiation oncologist at the U of A Medical Center to determine if the cancer had spread to any other part of the body. That would influence any treatment decisions, as well.

I stayed at home to work and take care of Hollis. Gene was met at the hospital by a couple of friends who lived close to the VA Medical Center. This couple went with him to the oncologist appointment to provide emotional support to Gene and take notes for me, which they emailed that same afternoon. Friends from our church drove him to the appointment. Our support system was assembling.

The oncologist confirmed the diagnosis, staged Gene's tumor, and referred him to the radiation department at the University of Arizona. The oncology resident we had met a few days earlier took over coordination of Gene's treatment. This resident was very aggressive in making appointments, getting Gene a place to stay as an outpatient in the hospice unit of the VA Medical Center, where he would stay five days a week, coming home only on weekends to rest before resuming treatments the next week. Having a resident who was taking such an active interest in Gene's case assured us that everything possible was being done for his care.

After that first appointment with the VA oncologist, our friends left Gene to wait for his ride back home and to email me with the answers to a list of questions I had sent with him. Gene waited five hours before calling me. A few minutes before his call, our priest called to tell me that the church friends who had given Gene a ride to the hospital had been in a serious automobile accident outside the VA Medical Center after they had dropped Gene off. The couple was hospitalized at another medical facility in the same city.

Gene was stranded, and the man who had driven him to his appointment was in intensive care. When Gene called, I told him to sit tight at the Life Support Unit. Hollis and I would be there to get him in two hours. After picking her up from a friend's house, we drove to the VA Medical Center, retrieved Gene, and got back home at about midnight. It had been a surreal day, and a pall of fear enveloped us as we all rode back home in silence. Was it an omen that the kind man who'd given Gene transportation to his first oncology visit was fighting for his life in another hospital? (This couple would eventually make it back home, but their stay in the hospital lasted for months.)

The Veterans' clubs in our little community agreed to provide transportation for Gene's weekly visits to and from the VA Medical Center. Each Monday, Gene would be taken to the VA Medical Center hospice. From there he would be transported to the U of A Radiation Center. His treatment would last about fifteen minutes, and he would wait for transportation back to the VA hospice, where he would rest in his room, take his meals, and wait for the treatment scheduled for the next day. Each Friday, he would come home for the weekend, to rest up for the set of treatments scheduled the following week. I noticed by the second treatment that when he would return from the radiation treatment and call me, his voice sounded weak and his words slurred.

During his first weekend at home, I was appalled at how he looked after his first three treatments. He had lost ten pounds already and wasn't sure what room of our house he was in or what he was supposed to be doing. He was disoriented for most of the visit home. The disorientation began to clear up by Sunday night, when it was time for him to return to the VA Medical Center for more radiation treatments. Every day his condition worsened. He got sores in his mouth and he refused to eat.

After a week of radiation treatments, the night shift found him wandering around the hospice facility in the middle of the night, disoriented and looking for me. ("My wife and only trusted friend," he told the nurse.) The next day the hospice nurse called me to report that they had found two bottles of medication in his personal belongings that Gene had not claimed during admission, which they had confiscated. My husband, a certified substance-abuse counselor who had been clean and sober for fourteen years and who had helped hundreds of alcoholics and addicts get clean, was re-addicted to sedatives and pain medication. He had taken a stash of medication with him to the hospital, which he declined to report when he was admitted, and was self-medicating in the middle of the night, on top of the medication that the nursing staff was giving him. I drove that night to the VA Medical Center with a heavy heart. It was clearly time for me to act on his behalf.

The hospice team at the VA hospital had assembled and we informed them that we wanted Gene titrated off the very addictive sedatives. It was two days before Thanksgiving. After nurses discovered him walking around in the middle of the night, Gene had slept almost twenty-four hours while they checked his vitals every half hour to make sure his overdose was not life threatening. The next day he sat by me on his bed, unsure of where he was. He held my hand and looked out into space. The hospice team was not sure it was in Gene's best interests to be slowly taken off the addictive medication. I looked at my husband and back at them.

"I don't think my husband wants to be in this condition," I said as I watched him drool, looking down at the floor. When we asked him directly, he was unable to say at that point what he wanted. Later that morning I met with the patient advocate. She was reminded of Gene's medical history concerning his tours in Vietnam and his subsequent history of drug addiction. She ordered that Gene be titrated off the addictive medication.

My husband had lost an additional twenty pounds since the beginning of radiation treatments, and a total of seventy pounds since the beginning of his first illness. Most of the time he was too weak to talk above a whisper or walk more than a few yards on his own. I called the U of A oncologist, who advised that I could not stop the radiation treatments without a court order or unless I had Gene judged incompetent and became his legal guardian. I wasn't willing to rob Gene of his right to choose.

By Thanksgiving, on a day pass, Gene was able to come to lunch with Hollis and me to a nearby restaurant. He was obviously detoxing from the medication, since he was jittery and irritable, but he knew who and where he was. He was grateful that I had confronted the medical team on his behalf, and he re-committed himself to his program of sobriety. That day, I asked Gene to stop the radiation treatments. He was clearly in turmoil and told me he thought it was his last chance at life. He wasn't ready to leave me, he said. How could he leave me, having just found me after waiting all his life?

The next week, so weakened by the radiation, Gene had to be taken to the VA van in a wheelchair after his treatment. He called me that afternoon and asked me to pick him up. He had told the U of A oncologist that he wanted the radiation treatments to stop and that he wanted to go home.

A rural veteran in our county had never been allowed to receive hospice care at home. With the cooperation of the patient's advocate and the VA Hospice team, Gene was discharged into the care of our local hospice program. We registered him into hospice on December 1, the weekend of my fiftieth birthday. He was fifty-six years old.

The Hospital Bed

Once home, Gene's condition began to improve. With daily calls from his AA sponsor, his recovery from his addiction was being managed, one day at a time.

We stood in the master bedroom, holding hands and looking from a window down into the street. Two men from the medical supply company were unloading a hospital bed. Gene and I looked at each other. "I'm not using that thing," he said.

"I know. We aren't ready yet," I said to him as softly as I could, trying to assure him that this latest acquisition from hospice didn't mean he was dying tomorrow.

The men yelled from the front door, "Where do you want it?" "Up the stairs," I called out from the head of the stairs.

Following my voice, they brought the bed up the stairs and into the master bedroom. I pointed towards a set of six windows.

"There. We've decided we want it up here."

"Most people want the bed downstairs," the younger man said. "Makes it easier on you, since there are so many stairs..." His voice trailed off.

"Well, we've decided to put it up here so Gene can look outside. When the pecan trees start greening, it's like a tree house up here." They began to put together the hospital bed.

"We have to instruct you on how to use the bed," the bigger man said, handing us a huge pamphlet and more papers to sign confirming we were in possession of the hospital bed. Gene looked away. More than ever, I was handling all the family business. I half listened as the man instructed us on how to use the bed-which switches made it rise, and how to make the head and feet move up and down. I signed the papers and quickly took the men downstairs to the front door. As they left, I took a big breath.

"It's not so bad," I said, walking back into the bedroom. Gene was resting on our bed, looking at the hospital bed.

"I'm never going to use it. I'm sleeping with you until one of us dies." He grinned at me. "Maybe we can use it as a place to fold the laundry up here!" It sat there, jutting into the middle of the room.

Sure enough, over the next few weeks, the hospital bed collected coats and shoes and folded laundry. One day, about a month after it had been delivered, I made the bed.

"Just for decorative purposes, honey," I said, assuring Gene as he watched me put on the mattress cover. "What kind of sheets do you want?" We walked to the linen closet together. Peering in and poking around the single-sized sheets, Gene laughed as he took out our daughter's old jungle sheets.

"These," he said smiling, handing them to me. So far, he'd managed not to touch the hospital bed. It was becoming a symbol of "the end" for both of us, and neither of us was ready for that. Using the jungle sheets, I made the bed, and it continued to serve as coat caddy and laundry table for the upstairs.

◆　◆　◆

One Friday, Gene woke earlier than usual. He went downstairs. When he came back into the room he was carrying a cup of coffee. Throughout our married life, he had awakened early and brought me coffee in bed. But over the past few weeks he had become too weak to pull himself up the stairs with a cup. This morning, he seemed more energetic than usual. He pulled out his "honey do" list from his bedside table while I sat up to drink my coffee.

"Well, baby, I've been remiss in my duties around the house. Today I want to go to the hardware store and get what we need to fix the breakfast table."

As good as his word, he came with me to the hardware store, then the grocery store and the post office. Back home, he hung a coat rack in the kitchen and fixed the breakfast table, chores he'd been putting off for months.

The week before, we had begun to battle his pain. With the help of the hospice team, we were learning to recognize the symptoms indicating when the pain was going to "grow" again, and the doctor and nurses were doubling his pain medication every few days. This particular Friday, the plan was to double his pain medication again. After taking the medication, Gene turned on the television to watch the Weather Channel.

"Looks like it's going to rain all day tomorrow. Better get over to the video store and rent some videos," he said to me and Hollis. Hollis jumped up and down.

"It's my turn," she squealed. "It's my turn to choose the movies." Rainy days were rare in the desert, but the rain was a call to sit together as a family and watch movies. It was becoming a family tradition.

The rain arrived on schedule Saturday morning. Hollis and I prepared for video day: popcorn, sodas, and, of course, M&Ms. When all was ready, I said to her, "Go get Gene, honey. Tell him we're ready." I waited. It was taking a long time. Where were they?

"I can't get him up, Mommy!" Hollis said, running back into the kitchen. "He's not waking up." Panic. Oh God, was he dead? I flew up the stairs and rushed to the bed. No, still alive. Good pulse, good color. He was sleeping soundly. I sat beside him on the bed and roused him. "Genie, are you okay?" He looked at me through groggy eyes. "Hmmnnn, yeah," he mumbled to me, "jus' tired...real tired." "I'll check on you later, honey. Do you need anything?" He was already asleep by the time I stood up.

I went upstairs to check on him after the first movie. I was becoming alarmed, since he had never slept so much, and I asked him if I should call the hospice. Aroused somewhat by my concern, he tried to sit up. "No, I don't think so. I'm just tired from yesterday, I think." It was time for more medication. I was torn. Were we overmedicating him? The medication wasn't supposed to make him groggy. The benefit of the medication was that it took the pain away without making the patient sleepy. I hesitated, then gave him the agreed-upon dosage.

"Genie, I'm going to call the hospice." As I punched in the numbers on the handset, my heart began to pound. We'd rarely called the hospice after hours. It had been two months into our hospice experience, and all was going very well. We still did our errands together, and only once had I used a respite care volunteer, to go to a movie. Even then, Gene had made dinner for the caregiver. I was sure we had upped the medication too quickly. That was the problem.

The nurse on call would have to do. Our case manager wasn't available, the answering service told me. The nurse on call knew me from my work in the community. I knew her as a friend, not just as a nurse.

"Linda?" she said as I answered the phone. The hospice answering service had paged her and told her who was calling.

"Yes," I said, my pulse beating in my head. "Delores, Gene is sleeping all the time. He won't wake up. Hasn't been up all day. I think we're overmedicating him." I went through the pain diary we were required to keep. Day by day, hour by hour, medicine by medicine. There was quiet on the other end of the phone. "Delores," I said again. "I think we're overmedicating Gene. He won't wake up."

"Well, maybe we are," she said, "but Linda, I think you need to consider that Gene has gone into another stage of his illness." Silence. A long silence.

"No, Delores, that isn't it. Just yesterday, we did all the errands around the house that were on his to-do list. Really, he's been fine. Would you call Lana and ask her what she thinks?" Lana was the clinical coordinator of the hospice program. Delores knew I was asking to go over her head and seek more advice.

"Yes, of course. I'll call her and I'll call you right back."

I sat on the bed next to Gene. He slept. Tears began to flow down my cheeks, and my panic grew. Every minute seemed like forever as I waited for her to call back. The phone rang. It was Delores.

"Lana says we can cut back on the medication, since it's been increased so many times already this week." I breathed and started to relax. She worked out the figure in her head. "She's going to call you, too, Linda."

"Thanks, Delores. I appreciate your calling back so quickly." Silence. "I know this must be very hard."

"Delores, really, everything is going very well. We've just overmedicated him, that's all." We hung up, and a few minutes later the coordinator called.

"Linda?"

"Yes."

"I wanted to call after I heard from Delores. We think Gene may have gone into another stage of his dying."

"No, Lana. Everything is fine."

"Linda?"

"Yes."

"If Gene wakes up tonight in pain, please give him the additional medication, okay?"

"Okay, of course. You know I'll do what you tell me to do. But I think everything's going to be fine now. I'll see Jill on Monday."

Gene slept all day Saturday, Saturday night, and Sunday. Monday, we saw our case manager.

The nurses regularly came into the house and up the stairs. There was no formal protocol for greeting them at the door. I heard her car door close and listened as she walked up the stairs. I searched her face when she came into the bedroom. Anxiety creased her face. In her gentle way, she came over to Gene's side of the bed and quietly pulled up a chair. He was awake, but still groggy.

"How're you doing, Gene?"

"I hurt," he whispered.

"Well, we're gonna take care of that for ya." Always kind and sweet, she spoke in her soft voice and assured him that all was well. "We're going to double the medication again, Linda," she said quietly to me, standing up. She walked towards the door, and I followed her.

"I'm shocked," she said. "I can't believe this is the same man I saw on Friday."

"I know. What's going on?" I desperately wanted to hear that my husband was just going through a temporary phase, that we still had many months together.

"We don't know yet," she replied, putting her arm around me. "But we're in this together. The main thing is to keep him out of pain."

"Yes, of course, but I don't understand," I said, crying. It's only been two months, Jill. And he's been doing so well. All the family errands with me. The chores. We just made cookies together on Thursday.

"I know. He's been remarkable. He's a remarkable man." She looked back at him; he was already asleep. "I'll drop the additional medication off this afternoon." She smiled, looking into my eyes, hugging me. "It might be time to turn on the oxygen for him," she said, looking at the oxygen concentrator by the bed. It had never been used. "It might make him more comfortable."

That night, Gene needed medication every two hours. I gave it to him as directed. He was restless, his arm and leg movements jerky with muscle spasms. He fought the oxygen, pulling the canula out of his nose.

I was exhausted on Tuesday morning as I sat by him on the bed. "Honey?" No answer. "Gene?" He roused and opened his eyes. Smiled at me. "Gene, I think we're going to have to move you to the hospital bed."

A firm "No." He added, "I want to be here."

"I know," I said as softly as I could. "I want you here, too. But Gene, in the middle of the night you accidentally hit me when you woke up. You know, when you were restless..."

"Oh no. I'm sorry." With a huge effort, he sat up. He looked at me, then at the hospital bed. He shut his eyes. With a deep sigh, he stood up and walked over to the hospital bed. He sat down, then lay between the sheets. The jungle sheets were still on the bed. I watched his face as he closed his eyes. Disappointment etched lines into his face. I pulled up a chair next to the hospital bed. As I held his hand, he slept.

Gene's Last Days

I awoke, startled and disoriented. There was a buzzing in my head. I didn't know where I was, but I knew I was exhausted. Was that a telephone ringing? Looking at the clock, which read... 11:30...P.M. I wondered about that as I answered the phone.

"Hello."

"How's my dad?" Mark was asking in my ear.

"Your dad," I said, looking over at the hospital bed. Suddenly my gut filled with dread. "Oh my God, Mark, he's not in the hospital bed!" I put down the phone, and as I ran around the bed I saw Gene sprawled on the floor in front of the closet. He was wet, and his arms were flailing as he tried to take off his wet jockey shorts, confusion flooding his face. I followed the trail of urine to the bathroom, where I found a puddle, and I then started to piece together what had happened. We were in a nightmare, a worsening nightmare from which we could never wake up. For two days I had been giving my husband pain medication every half-hour. His pain was out of control. The hospice team was doubling and quadrupling the dosage every day or two, trying to manage the terrible pain caused by his lung cancer. The day before, he had lost all motor control and become incontinent. And now, I had fallen asleep on the job. *Oh God,* I prayed urgently, *please help me.* I ran back to help Gene. I told him I'd be right there and assured him that everything was okay. I picked up the phone.

"Mark, your dad has scooched himself out of the hospital bed. I don't know how he did it. The railings are up. I've been asleep almost an hour and a half. I'm so sorry. I'm so tired. Your dad's in pain, and he's wet. I need to get him back in bed. Call me later and we'll talk.

And Mark, thanks for calling. He must have somehow been giving you guys the message to call, because he couldn't wake me up." Going back to Gene, I kept the prayers running full force. *I can't do this by myself, Lord. Please help me.*

"Please forgive me, Gene," I said as I changed him into clean shorts. He had been refusing to use the urinal. My marine-to-the-end husband would not give up control of his bladder to the cancer—or to the pain. He was dying—we knew that—but what we didn't know was how *close* he was.

"I want to go home," he whispered to me, looking directly into my face as he lay sprawled on the floor.

"Honey, I want you to go home, too," I said, holding him gently. He looked at me pleading, tears in his eyes.

"I want you to drive me."

"Genie," I said, knowing what he meant, "if we were meant to go together, we would have been killed on the road somewhere. Do you understand? Honey, I can't go with you. I have to stay here with Hollis." He nodded his head. "You told me last week your mom was coming to get you." He looked like he was understanding me, for the first time in days. "Well, she's coming to get you in a red '55 Chevy pickup." I remembered his favorite truck. "Have you seen her?" He nodded. "Well, next time you see her, you go with *her*. Okay?" He nodded again, exhausted.

Somehow, we got him back into the hospital bed. I knelt by him on the floor beside his bed, holding his hand. "Genie," I said, "I am so sorry. Can you ever forgive me for falling asleep? I am so sorry, Genie. I know you would never have fallen asleep with me in pain." He couldn't talk. His tongue no longer worked, and he never talked again. But he comforted me with his eyes. They told me not to be silly, there was nothing to forgive. I stayed awake the rest of the night. He lay there, his hands and feet clenched in pain. He couldn't swallow, and so, as directed, I put the liquid pain medication under his tongue every half-hour. He communicated with only his face. Turning toward me wherever I was in the room. Loving me. Comforting me. He had promised our daughter, Hollis, at our last family counseling meeting the week before, that he would not die while she was in the house. Her last request. Only one day to go before a friend would take her for a visit with her father in another city.

The hospice team came thirty minutes a day. During that time, I would rush to the bathroom for a shower then organize the household in another part of the house, away from Gene and the hospital bed. He wouldn't let them care for him anywhere below the waist. Modest until the end, my husband sought only my hand, my care. His anxiety lessened only when his eyes were locked into mine.

Two days after the phone call from Mark, a friend picked up our daughter for the visit to her father's home in Tempe. She picked Hollis up at five o'clock, after work. Hollis had said her goodbye the night before. "Gene, I love you. You have been a wonderful step-dad. I'll never forget you."

When the car pulled out of the driveway, I kneeled one last time by Gene's bedside.

"Honey, she's gone. She's gone to her dad's. Look for your mom, okay? It's okay. I'm going to be all right. I love you so much. You have been the most wonderful husband ever. And no one will ever replace you in my life. Go home, baby. I'll be with you as soon as I can."

His breathing changed then, becoming shallower over the next few hours. I was trying to read in the bed next to him. I watched him as his breaths evened out, then became fewer, and fewer, until at ten o'clock, five hours after Hollis had left, when he breathed his last breath. I looked at the bluish-white shell that had housed my husband—his eyes and mouth open, muscles slack, empty—and I heaved a sigh.

I called the priest, and I sat down to wait.

My Husband's Dream

One morning about a week before he died, Gene said to me, "I had a dream last night. We were two canvases. Huge, expensive canvases. And, as if by magic, brushstrokes were being spread, on your canvas and on mine. Luscious, rich colors.

I just remember that some colors were our strengths and some were our weaknesses. The strengths far outweighed the weaknesses. And our light was blinding. We are beautiful."

Epilogue

It's been five months since I loved and coached Gene through his death. "You helped Gene die well," one hospice nurse said, comforting me a few weeks after his death. She listened again to my story about the last days of his life.

Now I wake up from time to time feeling a tremendous pressure on my chest, tears squeezing out of my eyes. I've learned that there is no help for me through these days. I will feel dead in my heart and yet my skin will burn with grief all day. Nothing helps, and God knows I've tried everything. Talking about it, not talking about it, reading, writing, staying busy, sitting quietly. Those days are the worst.

I was numb after Gene's death. I have come to realize that the first two weeks were a great blessing. I didn't feel anything and was clear minded, as though biologically I had been designed to get through the paperwork, the decision making, and the farewell. It was after those two weeks that my skin started to burn with the "fire of grief"—that is how I've come to think of it. I'm convinced that it must be different for all my brothers and sisters, young and old, who've lost their loves. But as for me, my skin burns, and my heart is so heavy I can hardly get enough air in my lungs. When I awaken in the morning and my hands are on fire, I know it will be "one of those days." I don't want to think and I do want to *talk*, endlessly and mindlessly. I will be forever grateful for the friends and hospice workers who have listened to me talk for hours about Gene's death, about both the event itself and the last moments of his life. Bless them for their patience and compassion.

Two moments stand out for me from the time right after the memorial service. I will remember both of them for the rest of my life—for I was not finished with the frightening reality of death, nor was my daughter.

Two weeks after Gene's death, I was driving my daughter to a friend's house. I was going to leave her there and pick up her friend's mother to accompany me to a book study group. A few blocks from her house, I saw a fast-moving shadow run across the street in front of me and under the wheels of my car. I felt the thud, and in that moment was transported back to Gene's bedside. I had never run over an animal before. Turning on my emergency blinkers, but not moving the car for fear that I would do more damage, I got out of the car and behind my left rear wheel I saw a beautiful cat, still alive and moving its front paws. I opened the trunk of my car, took out the blanket I always keep there, and wrapped the cat in it. I was out of my mind with grief, sobbing uncontrollably as I carried the cat from house to dark and empty house, looking for its owners. As I walked, I could feel the warm lifeblood of the animal running onto my belly and down my legs. A truck stopped by my car and a woman asked me if I was okay.

"No!" I cried, tears running down my face, "it's dying, and I can't stop it!" She suggested I take it to the animal emergency hospital. She would call on her cell phone to alert them that someone was coming.

People are infinitely kind.

I put the cat into the back seat of my car and drove to the hospital. The cat was dead by the time I got there, a frozen grimace on its face, eyes staring. No one showed up to help. Hollis opened her car door and was yelling at me that I was acting crazy, so I got back into the car and drove to my friend's house. By this time, my friend had already gotten a ride to the book study, but her husband was home. In years of knowing him, I had never spoken to him directly before. I carried the cat up to him and placed it, still wrapped in the blanket, in his arms.

"I can't do any more, Ron," I told him. "Would you please bury this cat for me? I killed it, but I can't do any more." His face was filled with worry and compassion as he looked at my swollen face. He agreed to bury the cat. Hollis went inside to play with her friends and I continued on to the book study.

The second incident occurred within a month of Gene's death. I was talking on the phone with a friend when Hollis came rushing into my bedroom in a panic.

"He's dead, Mommy!" she cried. "He's dead!" She was dripping wet and frantically pulling off her wet clothes. Alarmed, I hung up the phone and went to her, putting my arm around her to comfort her, and asked her what had happened.

"I was swimming in the canal, Mommy. There was a little boy on the side and he was jumping rope. Next thing I knew he was floating by me. Somebody noticed his tennis shoes. Before that we just thought it was a log floating by." She was crying hysterically, trying to change into dry clothes. "We have to go back, Mommy," she sobbed, and by this time we could hear the shrill sirens of an ambulance wailing down our street. She quickly dressed and we walked to the canal, about half a block from our house. Hollis was never allowed in the canal water, and we talked every time we passed the canal about never getting into it when it was filled with water. But this day, a girlfriend had lured her in, and a young three-year-old boy had fallen into the canal and drowned. By the time we got to the canal, the street was clogged with an ambulance and several police cars. People were pouring out of their houses, and a young child ran to get the parents of the little boy who had drowned. We were about ten feet from the back of the ambulance, whose rear doors were open. The white-faced child was already lying on the gurney in the back. Hollis was hanging onto me and crying that there was nothing she could do. "He went right by me, Mommy," she was screaming, "and I couldn't reach him! I tried, Mommy, I tried!"

Within a month of Gene's death, in very traumatic ways, we were both reminded that death is out of our hands and beyond our control. We were brought back to visit that frightening place within ourselves where we were helpless to prevent Gene's death. Ultimately, we couldn't stop him from dying.

Every day I remind myself that I did the best I could to help Gene live a vibrant, happy life. I comfort myself with the knowledge that my husband felt loved and cherished. He knew I did everything in my power to make his final moments with us as pain free and worry free as possible. I helped my husband die well—it was the death he wanted, with as much dignity and peace as possible.

I am comforted to know that, in Gene's own words, my canvas is painted with more strengths than weaknesses. It is true of all of us— our strengths far outweigh our weaknesses, our lights are blinding. We are all beautiful.

The End

www.ingramcontent.com/pod-product-compliance
Lightning Source LLC
Chambersburg PA
CBHW051248120626
46547CB00014B/1843